SOMEWHERE to HIDE

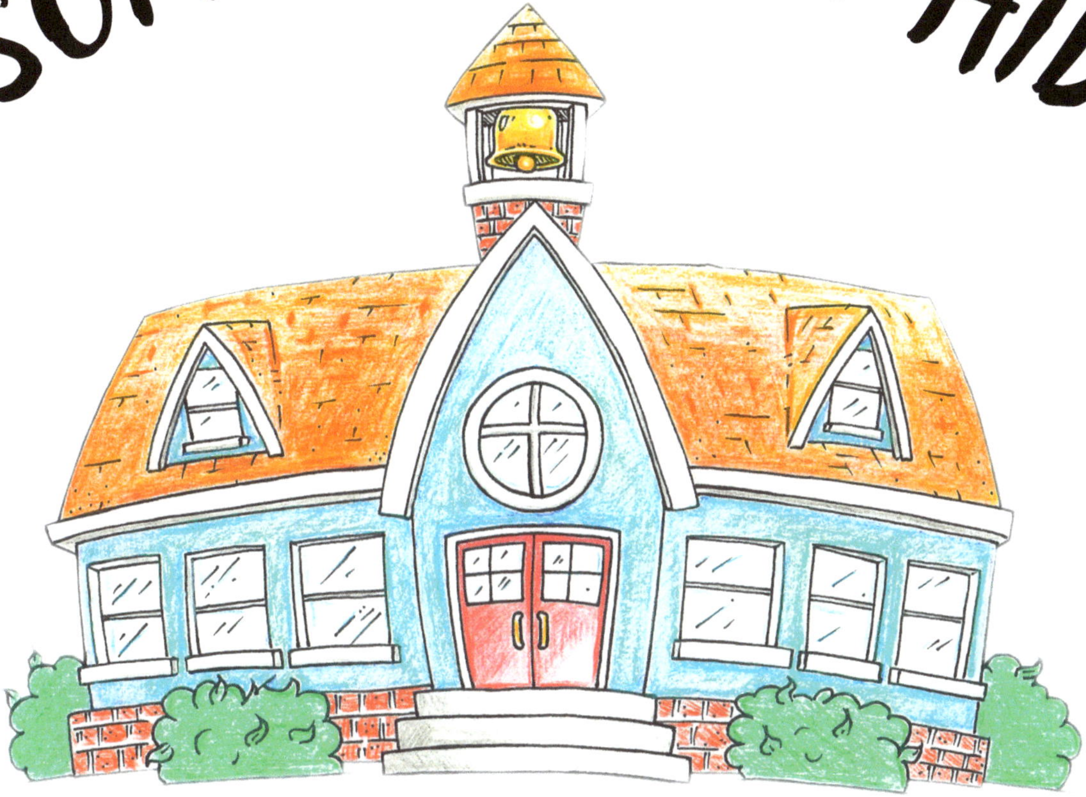

Written by Mireya DeYoung

Illustrations by Rhiannon Elise,
Jessica Gershin, and Arianna Gomez

Dedicated to all the schoolchildren in the United States of America, and in memory of all the children involved in these school shootings:

Robb Elementary School (Uvalde, Texas)

Sandy Hook Elementary School (Newtown, Connecticut)

Columbine High School (Columbine, Colorado)

Marjory Stoneman Douglas High School (Parkland, Florida)

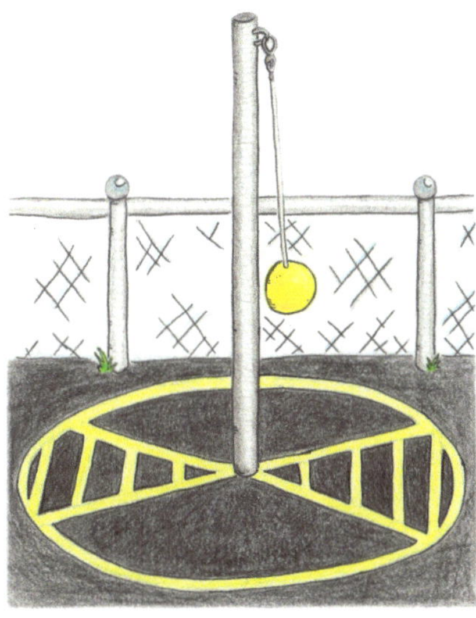

Author's Note to Parents

While all schools may have different words to describe a lockdown drill and its steps, all lockdown drills are generally the same. This book will be using a standard drill type procedure that may or may not be used by your child's school. However, it is important to know that the steps of the highest-level lockdown drill are the same regardless of the name, color, or number that is placed before or after it.

"Come in, class," Miss Mary said with a smile, pointing to the rug in the front of the classroom. "Let's put your things away and get settled down on the rug."

As the children sat down on the rug, Miss Mary said, "Let's cross our legs, crisscross like applesauce. Right, class?"

Miss Mary looked around at the children with a smile to see their excitement and nods of approval.

"Today, class, we're going to practice a very important drill," Miss Mary said while standing in front of the chalkboard.

Xavier raised his hand first while yelling out, "Are we going to practice a fire drill?"

Jamie then said, "What about an earthquake drill?"

Luke then yelled out proudly, "I know! A tornado drill!"

"Nope!" Miss Mary said as all the boys sighed at the same time. "None of those drills."

"Today, class, we're going to practice something called a lockdown drill," Miss Mary said.

"What's that?" the class started to whisper.

"Let's settle down, class," Miss Mary said while she continued.

DREAM BIG
What?
What's that?
Huh?

"The first type of lockdown is when the police or fire department is responding to an emergency outside of the school. At that time we will lock down the school and you will continue on with your studies in the classroom. You may also hear this type of lockdown be called *shelter-in-place*."

Lockdown Level 1
Lower Level Lockdown
GREEN

"If someone who can be considered dangerous or unsafe enters the school, a message will come over the loudspeaker or I will receive a direct message saying *The school is in lockdown* or *Barricade in place*."

"Now, before we go on with the steps I want to practice a song I wrote for you to all remember what to do."

LOCKDOWN SONG

Lock   lock   lock the door
Wait for the all clear
Now let's make our way out-side
Hug your friends and peers

After the class sang their new song, Miss Mary continued with steps of the lockdown drill.

"After I lock the door," she said, "I may place something in front of the door for extra safety."

"While all of the adults in the school are securing the doors and closing all of the blinds and windows so no one can see in or out," Miss Mary said, "you, class, have a very important job as well."

- Go to your safe space
- Stay hidden
- Stay still
- Stay very, very quiet

"If you find yourself in the bathroom and you can't get to a classroom, stay in place and follow these steps."

- Place anything you can in front of the door
- Enter a stall
- Lock the door
- Lift up your feet
- Stay very quiet
- Wait for your teacher, principal, or a police officer to get you out

"It is important for all of you to know we will not be able to open the classrooms once they are locked. We will do everything we can to get as many of you to safety as possible."

"If you find yourself in a hallway try to find the best safe space to hide that is not out in the open. It is very important to stay quiet wherever you are."

Miss Mary cleared her throat to break the silence as she looked around at all the students sitting quietly and said, "Class, let's sing our lock down drill song again."

LOCKDOWN SONG

Lock   lock   lock the door

Wait for the all clear

Now let's make our way out-side

Hug your friends and peers

Just as the class finished the last note of their song, Peter raised his hand.

"Yes, Peter?" Miss Mary asked.

Peter started to speak with a confused tone in his voice.

"Miss Mary, do we have to hide from all strangers who come into the school?"

"Oh no, Peter," Miss Mary said, looking around at the class. "Sometimes strangers will come into the school to fix something or meet with staff. Those may be strangers to you but not to the school or staff. We only use this drill if a stranger comes in that no one in the school knows, or if that stranger wants to be a danger to others. In the case that a person wants to be a danger to others we will lock the doors, close the blinds, go to our safe space, stay very quiet, and wait for the principal to give us the all clear."

Emma raised her hand.

"Yes, Emma?" Miss Mary said.

"What does *all clear* mean?" Emma said.

"That's a great question, Emma," Miss Mary said. "*All clear* means that the staff, principal or police have searched inside and outside the school, and the danger is no longer in or around the school. When someone says all clear, it means you can come out of your safe space and go outside of the school.

"Now, class, let's sing our song to practice what we need to do together."

LOCKDOWN SONG

Lock   lock   lock the door

Wait for   the   all   clear

Now let's make our way out-side

Hug your friends and   peers

Paula was the next student to raise her hand.

"Yes, Paula?" Miss Mary said.

"If a lockdown drill happens when you're not with us, what do we do?" Paula asked shyly. "Is someone going to hurt us?"

"Oh, Paula," Miss Mary said, "I understand that this topic can be hard to talk about but we must talk about it. We practice these drills to keep all of you safe in case a lockdown happens."

"All of us have big feelings about this drill. Some of us feel sad, worried, or even confused. That's okay. It is important for you to feel safe at school and not worry about this type of situation.

"However, if it comes up, we know what to do. If you're not with me in class, you are either going to go into lockdown where you are, or find the closest staff member, because we are all trained to keep you safe and get to a safe space. Remember to listen, breathe, and stay quiet."

"Now, class, the next thing I want to talk to you about is this bucket," Miss Mary said.

She pointed to a bucket sitting on her desk as she walked over to stand behind it.

"Class, if we ever need to go into a lockdown it is important for you to know we will not be able to leave the classroom. That means we will not be able to leave the classroom to use the bathroom. If anyone in the classroom needs to go to the bathroom while we are in lockdown, they will need to use this bucket."

"Eww!" the class said, while some giggled.

"I know it's not ideal," Miss Mary said, "but to keep you safe, we need to stay in the classroom. This will be the only way to use the bathroom at that time."

LIFE
OF A
PLANT
LOCKDOWN KIT
T-5 N.F.
TOILET
DEODORANT

From the back, Miss Mary heard a sniffle.

"What's wrong, Angel?" Miss Mary asked as she bent down to place her hand on Angel's shoulder.

Angel spoke softly. "Miss Mary, I'm scared."

"Oh, Angel," Miss Mary said. "I understand, and it's okay to be scared. This drill is scary for everyone, because we don't know what a lockdown would be like in real life. If we practice this drill and are aware of our surroundings, we'll be better prepared in case it happens at our school. But I hope it never does."

Max then asked, "Miss Mary, when can we stop practicing this drill?"

Miss Mary sighed.

"Max, that is a great question but a hard one to answer. I don't know that we ever will. Lots will need to change to stop this drill from needing to happen. A lot of grownups would need to agree on how we govern, and on laws about our health."

Mrs. Mary continued, "The one thing we can do to start the change is by being nice, patient, courageous, and brave, to and for one another. If you see or hear something that's not right, or if someone is having a problem, say something to a teacher, principal, or your parents. Be kind and be there for one another. I think the most important thing to do is to never talk bad about one another and include each other always. Those are the first steps you can take to try and make sure we all never have to find somewhere to hide."

What Questions
Do You Have?

Questions

Answers

Information about School Shootings

The United States of America is divided on how citizens can address school shootings. Until agreements can be made on how to handle them, parents and educators need to arm ourselves and our

children with knowledge of how to protect ourselves and prevent these needless acts of violence from continuing to happen to our most vulnerable population and within our educational system.

At the time of this book's publication (June 2023), there have been 24 school shootings in the United States, according to *Education Week*. While there still continues to be great debate and questions as to why and how this can continue to happen within our school system, our goal should not waver from protecting our most valuable and vulnerable community members: our children.

In the meantime, while everyone is trying to come to the best solutions to stop school shootings, there are a few things we can do to help our younger generations to become more prepared. Supporting our children by asking questions, answering questions, and just being available to them are great ways to let them know they can ask for help.

Encourage your child to always be kind and show empathy to others. Teach your child to be vigilant of their surroundings at all times. Always remind your child they are loved.

For more information, please visit

www.inspireyourchild.org

PUBLISHER'S NOTE

The drawing of the interior of US Capitol Building that appears on page 47 was completed by a fifteen-year-old up-and-coming artist, Arianna Gomez. Thank you, Arianna!

From now on, all Inspire Your Child LLC books will feature a young artist for at least one page of every book. For more information, or to inquire how to get your art into a book, please contact us at info@inspireyourchild.org, or through any of our social media platforms.

www.ingramcontent.com/pod-product-compliance
Lightning Source LLC
Chambersburg PA
CBHW041604110726
48005CB00002B/277